MW01179149

The Erin Nicole Simpson 204 Books Project and Science Scholarship Fund

In Memory of Erin Nicole Simpson
September 9, 1978 - August 14, 2019

"A Little Girl Who Loved to Read and Learn"

"I shall find out thousands and thousands of things - I shall find out about people and creatures and everything that grows - and the secret garden bloomed and bloomed and every morning revealed new miracles." Frances Hodgson Burnett

Our Mission:
"To see young women of science succeed, and young minds learning and well-read."

Contact:
Pam Simpson
Ens204book.sciencefund@gmail.com

Learning is Fun For Kids

Who Lives in My Garden?

Kim Banks

An Early Reader's Learning Book

Dreamstone Publishing © 2015

www.dreamstonepublishing.com

Copyright © 2015 Dreamstone Publishing and Kim Banks

All rights reserved.

No parts of this work may be copied without the author's permission.

ISBN-13:   978-1-925499-61-2

Other Books in the "Learning is Fun for Kids....." Series

Out Now

"Watch My Potatoes Grow"

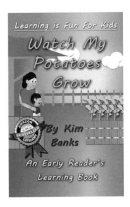

Coming Soon

"The Farm Field Trip"

"Cheering Up Eggplant"

This series is designed for early readers – Ages 4 to 8. The stories are fun, but educational, and are designed to encourage discussion and exploration.

Who Lives in My Garden?

In fall my mother let me start a garden in the back yard.

It's filled with all kinds of vegetables and berries.

We're even growing grapes!

But one thing that I never expected to find in my garden was tons and tons of bugs.

So many bugs.

I've lost count!

Each one is unique.

Each one does something for my amazing garden.

First there is the garden
spider.

We've had many build
their webs in my garden!

They eat the flies and
other bugs that try to eat
my veggies.

Second is the butterfly.

We get new ones each day it seems.

From the Monarch to the Red Admiral they are beautiful.

And there are even tiny moths that bring joy as they fly past.

Third there are amazing beetles.

I have seen stag beetles, church beetles and mealworm beetles.

Each one is peaceful, but they do try hard to eat my veggies.

Fourth is the garden snail.

Sometimes they are good and sometimes bad.

They love it when I water my plants and they get to drink it too.

They eat my plants at night, and I see their silvery trails on the path in the morning!

Fifth is the bumble bees.

They love the flowers on my plants.

They are large and peaceful but when I tried to grab one, its sting hurt like crazy!

I won't do that again!!

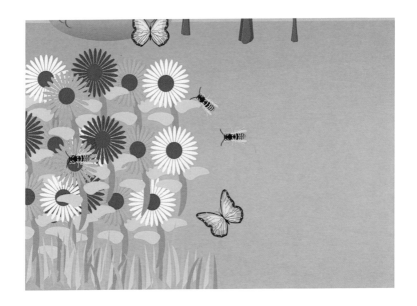

Sixth is the ladybug.

My grandfather said that they bring good luck to plants, and to people, so we have plenty of luck in our garden.

Seventh is the dragonfly.

They don't come around often, but when they do, they are amazing to watch and admire from afar.

They love the little pond we made in my garden.

Eighth is the garden ants.

If I miss picking the ripe veggies, the next day I find a row of ants all around the fallen food.

Even when it's all rotten and squishy, they seem to enjoy it.

There are thousands and thousands of ants.

I tried to count them once, but there were too many!

Ninth is the earthworms.

They are peaceful and slow, but they eat any leaves that fall off my veggies when I'm not looking.

They help the dirt to stay clean and fresh, and eat all the dead leaves too - so we keep them around.

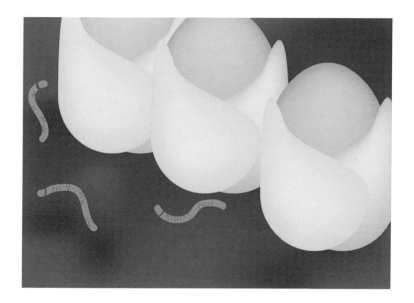

Tenth is the crickets.

They make noise all night with their chirpy singing.

My mother says that they sing because they want to find a mate.

With all of those insects in my garden, how is there room for my plants to grow!?

Thank You For Buying This Book!

I hope that you have enjoyed it.

Please leave us a review and let us know what you thought!

Leaving reviews helps other readers discover good books.

ABOUT THE AUTHOR

Kim Banks is a mother who gave up her corporate job to work from home.

She enjoys writing of all kinds, but is most passionate about creating books that encourage kids to read, and to learn, and to have fun doing it!

Other Books from Dreamstone Publishing

Dreamstone publishes books in a wide variety of categories – here are some of our other bestselling books:-

How to Bake the Best

Delicious Valentine's Day

Cupcakes - In Your

Kitchen

By Kim Lambert

How to Bake the Best

Delicious Easter Cupcakes

and Sweet Treats - In

Your Kitchen

By Kim Lambert

(Also available in Spanish)

The "How to Bake the Best……" Series.

All Books available from all Amazon sites and other good book stores, and available for Kindle too!

How to Bake the Best

Delicious Christmas

Cupcakes and Muffins -

In Your Kitchen

By Kim Lambert

How to Bake the Best

Delicious Fudge For All

Seasons - In Your Kitchen

By Kim Lambert
and Charly Leetham

Be the first to know when our next books are coming out

Be first to get all the news – sign up for our newsletter at

http://www.dreamstonepublishing.com

CPSIA information can be obtained
at www.ICGtesting.com
Printed in the USA
LVRC020057131118
596934LV00010B/180

* 9 7 8 1 9 2 5 4 9 9 6 1 2 *